I Said No!

A kid-to-kid guide to keeping private parts private

by Zack and Kimberly King

Illustrated by Sue Ramá

Prologue by Chip St. Clair

Preface by Sandra L. Caron, Ph.D.

Boulden
publishing

Boulden Publishing

P.O. Box 1186

Weaverville, CA 96093

www.bouldenpublishing.com

Designed and edited by Sue Ramá

Manufactured in China

June 2012 Edition

ISBN-13: 978-1-878076-49-6

10 9 8 7 6 5 4 3 2

Boulden
publishing

Helping you help kids.

Contents

Prologue

This is a unique and valuable tool, written to give the child in your life a set of guidelines for handling a variety of situations and the understanding that there is always a trustworthy adult to call upon for help. I consider it a privilege to write the preface for such a well structured, wonderfully written, and thoughtfully designed book. It is fresh and smart, without the overtones of dread or despair that so often shadow this topic, and I believe had the precepts outlined been introduced to me as a child, a profound and lasting impression would have been made.

Of all this world's beauty and miracles, brilliance and simplicity; of all of nature's graces, children are truly the most remarkable, great sponges just waiting to soak up new information, experience new feelings, and explore new ideas. They stare out at this incredible world of ours in awe and wonderment, eager to learn and understand without prejudice or cynicism. If an adult can learn, can remember how to engage all that surrounds and all that is within through the eyes of a child, well mankind may just reclaim the lost paradise written about by Milton.

Properly harnessed and directed, a child will grow and laugh and love with confidence, resilience, and passion. They will be armed with optimism and tenacity when facing life's normal challenges. Yet there are particular challenges children are sometimes faced with that threaten to shatter their innocence. Too often challenges are unaddressed until after a situation arises, leaving children frightened and unsure of what to do. Left unchecked, those feelings can haunt them into adulthood, undermining their security, confidence, and coping abilities.

I know firsthand the struggles of guilt and fear that consume a suffering child. Teachers, friends, neighbors — no one would have known what I locked away behind my eyes. Through my work and endeavors like this book, children can be helped and we can all journey towards a beautiful world where children's beauty and innocence can thrive.

Chip St. Clair

Chip St. Clair is the author of *The Butterfly Garden* and a regional director of Justice For Children.

For more information about *The Butterfly Garden* go to www.butterflygardenmemoir.com

For more information about Justice For Children go to www.jfcadvocacy.org.

Preface

Curiosity is natural. Young children discover that they are different and curiosity and exploratory behavior are a natural response. There are real dangers such as adults who abuse children and even older children who take advantage of younger children. This book is intended to teach children how to recognize people who might potentially be dangerous without discouraging normal exploration. By accepting children's natural curiosity about sexuality and gender differences as normal and healthy, parents build a basis for positive attitudes toward sexuality. Parents also need to teach their children how to recognize real danger.

Sandra L. Caron, Ph.D.

Sandra L. Caron, Ph.D is a professor of Family Relations and Human Sexuality at the College of Education and Human Development, University of Maine

Note from the author: Reading this book in its entirety in one sitting may prove overwhelming for your child; particularly a younger child. I would like to recommend an approach that was successful with my youngest. We read a section at a time, took time to discuss it and then put it away for another day.

— *K. K.*

Dedication

To my wonderful family, I love you all very much. I am so proud! — Grazie

To Sue Ramá, illustrator, editor and writer! Working with you on this project has been a joy! Your knowledge, advice, honesty and true understanding of this story made our story so much better!! Your editing and suggestions were essential in the success of this project.

You took my manuscript and made it shine. Thank You. —KK

To Zack, who generously shares his story so other children may learn and stay safe. Yay, Zack! You're a hero!

To Barbara Lavey, a heroine. — S R

My name is Zack
and this is my mom.

I had a not so good time at a
sleepover party last year.

Mom always said, "Keep your
privates. . .private!"

1

SO, WHAT ARE "PRIVATES?"

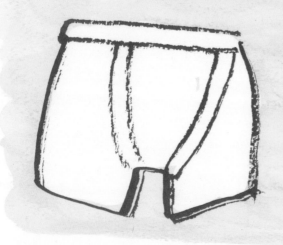
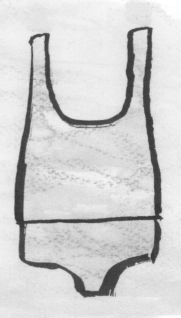

Private parts for boys are the parts of your body that are under your underwear.

Private parts for girls are the parts of your body that are under your underwear and undershirt.

There are doctor names and lots of other names for your private parts!

We are sure you have heard of a few of them!

You might want to talk about some of those names now.

Your body is a wonderful thing!

It is important to keep it healthy, safe and clean.

It is important to learn about your body.

When you are a kid, learning about the world, it's natural to be curious about bodies. Say you are a boy like me, my mom says that it is natural to be a little curious about what girls bodies look like. Or if you are a girl with no brothers you might be curious about what boys look like.

But Mom says that once you are not a baby anymore, privates just stay private. Mom says that this is called modesty.

Maybe you are a little curious about the differences between girls and boys.

You might want to talk about your curiosity now.

3

SOME SPECIAL RULES

There are some special rules to learn about your private parts that are super importanto! My mom and I are going to talk about them now. These rules can help you stay safe and feel good about yourself!

Because your private parts are meant to be private, there are only a few people besides yourself who should see and touch them.

When you are a baby, the grownups that take care of you have to wipe your private parts to keep them clean and healthy. Your mom and dad have to clean up the mess from your dirty diapers. Of course they also give you baths, because you could not do that for yourself.

When you are a little dude, like two or three, you are learning to go potty!*

*These are the words we use in our house, but if you use different words, that's okay!

4

When you are learning how to do that, sometimes mom or dad might have to help you wipe yourself to keep your private parts clean. Of course, that is okay. They are helping you and teaching you to take care of yourself.

Sometimes you might go to the doctor for a checkup.

If your mom or dad is in the room with the doctor then it is okay for the doctor to examine your private parts. The doctor wants to make sure that all of the parts of your body are healthy.

But parents, caregivers, doctors and you are the only people who ever need to see, clean, or examine your private body parts. (Examine is a big word and here means to look at.)

Parents, caregivers and doctors are what we like to call green flag people. It's okay for green flag people to see your private parts when they are taking care of you.

You may have other green flag people who are allowed to help take care of you in these ways. Why don't you talk about who those people are right now.

RED AND GREEN FLAGS

What do I mean by green flag people?

So that I can remember all of this important stuff, I imagine something funny in my brain.

Imagine a ship sailing on the ocean and a funny little sailor. The funny little sailor is putting a green flag up over his ship! The ship that sails with the green flag on the ocean means all is safe, there are gentle seas!

Everything is okay.

You feel safe and comfortable.

You are happy.

Smooth sailing ahead!

7

But a red flag is raised on
a ship when there are
dangerous seas ahead.

RED means BAD!
RED means STOP!

RED is DANGER!

Red flags should go up
on your ship if you are
with someone and you
find yourself feeling:

UPSET

UNCOMFORTABLE

LONELY

SAD

ANGRY

SCARED

YUCKY

IN DANGER!

If people who are not taking care of you want to see or touch your private parts, or if they want you to see or touch their private parts, *put up a red flag!*

10

If kids or other grown-ups offer you things like candy, money or toys to look at or touch your privates ***put up a red flag!***

When kids or other grown-ups offer you stuff and ask you to look at or touch their privates ***put up a red flag!***

If you get that feeling inside that something like this just isn't right, even if somebody else tells you it is, ***put up a red flag!***

SAY NO!

Those feelings are called instincts.

Follow your instincts!

SAY NO!

TREATS, BRIBES AND THREATS

Sometimes, a teacher might offer you a lollypop for doing a great job listening, or a neighbor might give you a cookie just to be friendly. That's okay!

These are rewards or treats and they are just fine.

12

But a bribe is different. A bribe is when somebody offers you money or prizes to do something for them that you really don't want to do.

If somebody tries to bribe you into doing something that involves "privates" put up a red flag.

If someone offers you a bribe, even if it is something great, don't take it.

Put up a red flag!

You might want to talk a little bit now about the difference between rewards or treats and red flag bribes.

WHAT IFS

If your friend, brother, sister, cousin, uncle, aunt, grandparent, teacher, coach, stranger or anybody else… Asks you if they can see your privates or touch your privates…

They might say, "If you keep this a secret I will buy you things!"

They might say, "If you keep this secret I will be your best friend"…

What should you think?
What should you say?
What should you do?

SAY:
DANGER, RED FLAG!

SAY: "No! No way!"
Be loud and clear!

DO: Get the heck out of there!

Tell your mom or your dad something happened that was very bad!

If a friend, relative, caregiver, or anyone… Asks you to look at or touch their privates…

What should you think?
What should you say?
What should you do?

THINK:
DANGER, RED FLAG!

SAY: "No! No way!"
Be loud and clear!

DO: If you can, get the heck out of there!

Tell your mom or your dad something happened that was very bad!

15

If you are in the bathroom at school and someone tries to touch your privates or wants you to touch his...

What should you think?
What should you do?
What should you say?

THINK:
DANGER, RED FLAG!

SAY: "No! No way!" Be loud and clear!

DO: Get the heck out of there!

Tell your teacher really quick.

Your teacher will tell your parents something happened that made you very uncomfortable.

16

If you are on the bus and someone dares you to pull down your underwear and she says she will give you $50 bucks...

What should you think?
What should you do?
What should you say?

THINK:
DANGER,
RED FLAG!

Underwear is supposed to stay on!

When somebody offers you money that is a bribe!

If you are at home with a babysitter and she says she wants you and your sister to play "Show and Tell" and look at your private parts…
What should you think? What should you do? What should you say?

THINK:
DANGER, RED FLAG!

SAY: "No! No way!"
Be loud and clear!

DO: Get the heck out of there if you can!

When your parents get home make sure to tell your mom and dad something happened that was very bad!

Maybe you would like to talk about a safety plan now.

THREATS

Some red flag people really stink!

They don't want anyone to know what they did.

So some red flag people don't tell the truth!

So, if a person has touched your privates, or they made you touch them… first they might try to bribe you, but they might also lie or threaten you.

They might say, "If you tell nobody will ever believe you, you are just a kid!"

They might say, "If you tell I will never be your friend ever again!"

Some threats can be really scary for a kid.

People who threaten kids are using their words to scare you into keeping quiet or keeping secrets. If you keep the secret they stay out of trouble. If you keep the secret they can do it again, to you, or to someone else.

19

If someone threatens you and you feel scared, wait until you are alone with a trusted adult, then be brave and tell that person about it.

Even if you feel funny about what happened. Even if you feel embarrassed by what happened. Remember it was not your fault, no way! You are just a kid.

Can you think of anything else a red flag person might say?

Can you think of an example of a bribe ?

Can you think of an example of a threat?

When I went to my first ever sleepover party with my best friend, and he said, "Did you know that all cool kids touch each others privates?"

That was a big lie!

He said "if you don't touch mine, I'll never be your friend again."

That was a threat!

I thought:

**DANGER
RED FLAG!**

Private parts are not for
sharing with friends!

I SAID NO!

NO WAY!
I was loud and clear!

I got the heck out of there!

I told his mom that her
kid did something really bad!

22

But, what if that mom doesn't help you… what should you do?

Think of a new plan that will help you!

My friend's mommy sent me back to the room with my red flag "friend." So, I decided to pretend to get a terrible stomach ache! I stayed in the bathroom by myself until it was really late, until everyone fell asleep!

I was proud of my plan and I thought I did great!

My mom thinks so too.

If somebody does make you feel unsafe, uncomfortable, alone, frightened or sad by something they have said or done to you, remember:

It is not your fault.

You should tell a grown-up about it.

There will always be somebody who will help you.

The people who take care of you need to know what happened to you.

If, for some reason you just can't tell your parents or your caregivers…

Who can you tell?

You can tell a trusted adult like:

OTHER ADULT RELATIVES, your aunt or your uncle, for example

NEIGHBORS

THE POLICE

FIREMEN OR FIREWOMEN

TEACHERS

ADULT FRIENDS

EMERGENCY OPERATORS (911)

Tell Someone.

Even if you think it isn't a big deal. Even if you are scared! Even if you think that they may not believe you!

Even if you feel embarrassed, tricked, or dumb... please be sure to tell.

Tell Someone You Trust.

Telling makes it stop!

Telling will help you to feel better too.

SECRET = RED FLAG

There should be no secrets between you and the people you love and trust. Tell your mommy, daddy, grandma, pop pop or whomever you trust if any thing like a red flag thing happens, even if you got away before anything even happened. Tell them everything!

Remember that Mom and Dad and all the people that love you are there to help. **They love you no matter what!**

You are loved and nobody has the right to hurt you!

Nobody!

The people who really love you want to protect you and help you.

28

I want to help other kids know what to do if a red flag thing starts to happen, or happens to them.

That is why my mom and I have written this book.

I went to my first sleepover party and had a red flag!

I know now that it happens to lots of kids.

I know it can happen to anyone.

So, if it does, remember, it isn't your fault.

I felt way better after I told my mom.

I feel even better now that I am telling you in this book!

We hope that if you read this book before a play date, a sleepover, or a day at the park… it will help you know what you can do to help yourself stay safe.

And…

If you read this book after a red flag thing happens you might feel better knowing that you aren't the only one out there that this has happened to! If you know there are lots of other kids that this has happened to, you might find more courage to tell!

I really hope so.

30

One more "What if…"

What if…

You have a parent or caregiver who has touched your privates, or made you touch theirs?

What if the red flag is up for them?

This is the hardest "What If" to understand.

If this happens it can be very confusing and really hard to know what to do.

You will have to be extra brave and tell somebody else that you trust.

Tell a trusted adult.

You might want to think about who you have in your life that you really, really trust. Why don't you think about that for a moment right now.

And remember, keep telling until somebody listens! It is very, very important.

If you can't get someone to listen to you,

If they don't pay attention to what you say,

If they don't believe you and take steps to keep you safe, then…as soon as you can, as soon as you are safe…

pick up the phone and dial

911

and tell them!

That should always work! They have to listen at 911. It is their job! They will send someone to help and protect you.

This is a page for you to write and illustrate the green or red flag people in your life.

These are pages for you to help us finish our story with a "What if" illustration and story of your own.

Thank you for helping us finish our story!

Special Information for Caregivers

Afterword

When he was 5 years old, my son Zack had an experience that all parents wish their child would never have. At a birthday sleepover party Zack's best friend tried to engage him in inappropriate behavior that was beyond the realm of normal sexual curiosity for children.

I thought I had prepared Zack so that this could not happen to him. I considered myself a good mother and a good teacher of children, especially my own. I had been a kindergarten teacher for years and I had plenty of experience with my own three children.

I thought all my kids had enough information. How could they not? We had read books and we had talked about the subject. I had assumed that if my son or daughter was ever in a bad situation they would just say "NO!" or run away and that would be that.

I was wrong. I had talked to them too generally about this, missing the specifics which are required for this topic. I had neglected rehearsing different scenarios, even though my experience with young children had taught me that this is the way they learn.

Zack encountered more than we had talked about. Perhaps the most unexpected and scariest part was his best friend was capable of such behavior. We had known this family for years!!

I had not prepared him for the lies: "All the cool kids do this, Zack."

He was not prepared for blackmail, intimidation or threats: "Zack, if you tell... nobody will believe you!"

He was not prepared for bribery: "If you do this... I will give you 50 dollars."

All of these were used by his "best friend".

Zack felt uncomfortable, unsafe, and trapped; and the whole time he was literally right next door!

Once Zack realized he was in a bad situation, he tried many problem solving techniques. He told his friend's mom her child was doing weird things. She didn't really listen to his concerns.

He told his sister who was also at the party.

She went to the mom who just sent everyone back to bed!

He tried leaving the house by the back door. However, the doors were locked.

Finally, he said he had a stomach ache and locked himself in the bathroom where he was safer.

When I picked him up in the morning, my son collapsed in my arms and told me the story of his long and scary night. I was so very proud of him for the way he told me. And I was impressed to learn that he had managed to avoid this very inappropriate situation using his own creativity.

Following this event, Zack went through a period of confusion and depression. Six months of counseling and a lot of understanding were required. But four years later, Zack and the entire family is happy, healthy, and has moved on. We believe that this is in part because we wrote this book together.

One thing I learned, working on this project, is how widespread these events are in our children's lives. Zack and I, and our whole family, very much hope that our story will help you and many others prepare our little ones for situations they may encounter!

Kimberly King

Kimberly King is a kindergarten teacher with a Master's Degree in Early Childhood Education from Wheelock College, Boston

RESOURCES

Excellent information on sexual abuse prevention and support can be found at:

www.stopitnow.org

Darkness2light.com

1-800-PREVENT

www.jfcadvocacy.org

We will be donating a portion of our book sales to the organization Darkness To Light.